Seasons of Light

Thomas Kinkade

HARVEST HOUSE PUBLISHERS
EUGENE, OREGON 97402

Seasons of Light

Copyright © 1998 Media Arts Group, Inc.
San Jose, CA 95131
and Harvest House Publishers
Eugene, Oregon 97402

ISBN 1-56507-924-8

Media Arts Group, Inc.
521 Charcot Avenue
San Jose, CA 95131
1.800.366.3733

Scripture quotations are taken from the New King James Version,
Copyright © 1979, 1980, 1982 by Thomas Nelson, Inc., Publishers.
Used by permission.

Harvest House Publishers has made every effort to trace the ownership
of all poems and quotes. In the event of a question arising from the use
of any poem or quote, we regret any error made and will be pleased to
make the necessary correction in future editions of this book.

Printed in the United States of America.

Design and production by:
Koechel Peterson & Associates
Minneapolis, Minnesota

98 99 00 01 02 03 04 05 06 07 /IP/ 10 9 8 7 6 5 4 3 2 1

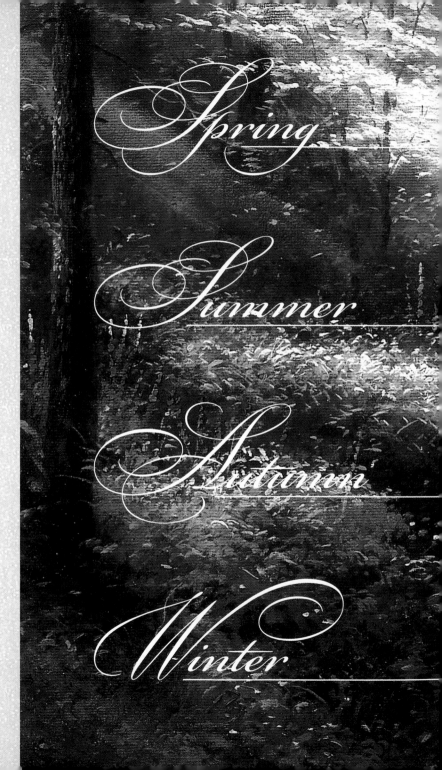

Spring

Summer

Autumn

Winter

To everything there is a season,

A time for every purpose under heaven. . . .

The Book of Ecclesiastes

Spring

Consider the lilies

of the field,

how they grow;

they neither toil

nor spin:

yet I tell you,

even Solomon

in all his glory

was not arrayed

like one of these.

The Book of Matthew

Spring

The skipping-rope was a wonderful thing.

She counted and skipped,

and skipped and counted,

until her cheeks were quite red,

and she was more interested than

she had ever been since she was born.

The sun was shining and

a little wind was blowing—

not a rough wind,

but one which came in

delightful little gusts and brought a

fresh scent of newly turned earth with it.

Frances Hodgson Burnett
The Secret Garden

*M*ore than half a century has passed,

and yet each spring, when I

wander into the primrose wood

and see the pale yellow blooms,

and smell their sweetest of scents

. . . for a moment I am seven

years old again and wandering

in the fragrant wood.

Gertrude Jekyll

Spring 9

Banks of gorgeous flowers were on every hand,

and birds with rare and brilliant plumage

sung and fluttered in the trees and bushes.

A little way off was a small brook,

rushing and sparkling along between green banks,

and murmuring in a voice very grateful

to a little girl who had lived so long

on the dry, gray prairies.

L. Frank Baum
The Wizard of Oz

*O*f all the wonderful things in the wonderful universe of God,

nothing seems to me more surprising than the planting of a seed

in the blank earth and the result thereof.

Celia Thaxter

*T*he wind in the night had blown away the last clouds; the sky was

everywhere a deep blue, and in the midst stood the sun,

shining on the green mountain; all the blue and yellow flowers

opened their cups and looked up with gladness.

Heidi jumped here and there and shouted for joy;

for there were whole troops of delicate primroses together,

and yonder it was blue with gentians, and everywhere in the

sunshine smiled and nodded the tender-leaved golden rockroses.

Johanna Spyri
Heidi

Spring 13

Spring is coming, spring is coming,

Birdies, build your nest;

Weave together straw and feather,

Doing each your best.

Spring is coming, spring is coming,

Flowers are coming too:

Pansies, lilies, daffodillies,

Now are coming through.

Spring is coming, spring is coming,

All around is fair:

Shimmer and quiver on the river,

Joy is everywhere.

Children's May Song

Summer

August creates

as she slumbers,

replete and

satisfied.

Joseph Wood Krutch

The clean, bright, gardened townships spoke of country fare and pleasant summer

evenings on the stoop. It was a sort of paradise.

Robert Louis Stevenson

Pollyanna had made a wonderful discovery—against this window

a huge tree flung great branches. To Pollyanna they looked

like arms outstretched, inviting her.

Suddenly she laughed aloud. "I believe I can do it," she chuckled.

The next moment she had climbed nimbly to the window ledge.

From there it was an easy matter to step to the nearest tree branch.

Then, clinging like a monkey, she swung herself from limb to limb

until the lowest branch was reached.

Eleanor H. Porter
Pollyanna

Summer 19

Saturday morning was come, and all the summer world was bright and fresh,

and brimming with life. There was a song in every heart;

and if the heart was young the music issued at the lips.

There was cheer in every face and a spring in every step.

The locust trees were in bloom and the fragrance of the blossoms

filled the air. Cardiff Hill, beyond the village and above it,

was green with vegetation; and it lay just far enough away

to seem a Delectable Land, dreamy, reposeful, and inviting.

Mark Twain
The Adventures of Tom Sawyer

Thomas Kinkade

A drop fell on the apple tree,

Another on the roof,

A half a dozen kissed the eaves,

And made the gables laugh.

A few went out to help the brook,

That went to help the sea.

Myself conjectured, were they pearls,

What necklaces could be.

Emily Dickinson

23

Summer

Summer afternoon—summer afternoon; to me those have always been

the two most beautiful words in the English language.

Henry James

Is there anything more soothing than the quiet whir

of a lawnmower on a summer afternoon?

F. Scott Fitzgerald

Summertime

And the livin' is easy,

Fish are jumpin'

and the cotton is high.

Ira Gershwin

Anne had the golden summer

of her life as far as freedom

and frolic went. She walked,

rowed, berried and dreamed

to her heart's content . . .

Lucy Maud Montgomery
Anne of Green Gables

Thomas Kinkade

Autumn

What moistens the lip

and what brightens the eye?

What calls back the past,

like the rich pumpkin pie?

John Greenleaf Whittier

Autumn

The year which is drawing toward its close has been filled with

the blessings of fruitful fields and healthful skies. . . .

I do, therefore, invite my fellow citizens . . .

to set apart and observe the last Thursday of November

next as a day of thanksgiving and praise to our

beneficent Father who dwelleth in the heavens.

Abraham Lincoln
October 3, 1863

Thomas Kinkade

Autumn 31

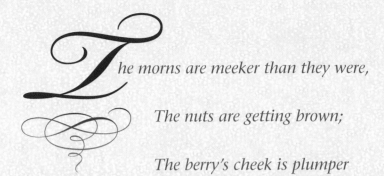

The morns are meeker than they were,

The nuts are getting brown;

The berry's cheek is plumper

The rose is out of town.

The maple wears a gayer scarf,

The field a scarlet gown.

Lest I should be old-fashioned,

I'll put a trinket on.

Emily Dickinson

Oh, Marilla," Anne exclaimed one Saturday morning, coming dancing in with her arms

full of gorgeous boughs. "I'm so glad I live in a world where there are Octobers.

It would be terrible if we just skipped from September to November, wouldn't it?

Look at these maple branches. Don't they give you a thrill—several thrills?"

Lucy Maud Montgomery
Anne of Green Gables

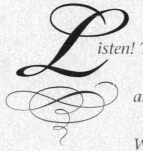

isten! The wind is rising,

and the air is wild with leaves,

We have had our summer evenings,

now for October eves!

Humbert Wolfe

Autumn

Season of mists and mellow fruitfulness,

Close bosom-friend of the maturing sun;

Conspiring with him how to load and bless

With fruit the vines that round

the thatch-eaves run.

John Keats

37

Autumn

Winter

Then God said,

"Let there be lights in

the firmament of the

heavens to divide the

day from the night;

and let them be signs

and seasons for

days and years. . . ."

The Book of Genesis

CHRISTMAS
OPEN
HOUSE

Thomas
Kinkade

The first fall of snow is not only an event but it is a magical event.

You go to bed in one kind of a world and wake up

to find yourself in another quite different,

and if this is not enchantment,

then where is it to be found?

J. B. Priestley

How the snowballs flew!

Almanzo ducked and dodged and yelled,

and threw snowballs as fast as he could,

till they were all gone.

Laura Ingalls Wilder
Farmer Boy

The snow piled against the window was not like other snows.

The wind in the chimney was not like other winds.

If you scratched a frosted place out of which to look,

you saw that the snowpacked prairie to the north

was a white country in which no other person lived,

that the snowpacked timberland to the south

was a white woods forever silent.

It was as though there were no humans

at all in any direction but your own family.

Bess Streeter Aldrich

Thomas
Kinkade

Christmas morning broke on a beautiful white world. It had been a very mild

December and people had looked forward to a green Christmas;

but just enough snow fell softly in the night to transfigure Avonlea.

Anne peeped out from her frosted gable window with delighted eyes.

The firs in the Haunted Wood were all feathery and wonderful;

the birches and wild cherry-trees were outlined in pearl;

the ploughed fields were stretches of snowy dimples;

and there was a crisp tang in the air that was glorious.

Lucy Maud Montgomery
Anne of Green Gables

Winter is the time for comfort, for good food and warmth,

for the touch of a friendly hand

and for a talk beside the fire:

it is the time for home.

Edith Sitwell

Winter 47

PAINTINGS